People Around the World

Life and Culture in
AUSTRALIA
AND THE PACIFIC REALM

J. M. KLEIN

PowerKiDS
press™

Published in 2021 by The Rosen Publishing Group, Inc.
29 East 21st Street, New York, NY 10010

First Edition

Editor: Siyavush Saidian
Book Design: Seth Hughes

Photo Credits: Cover Anton Balazh/Shutterstock.com; p. 5 Peter Hermes Furian/Shutterstock.com; p. 7 TORSTEN BLACKWOOD/AFP/Getty Images; p. 8 (top) Saruman-the-white/Wikimedia Commons; p. 8 (bottom) Lisa Maree Williams/Stringer/Getty Images News/Getty Images; p. 9 Wade Davis/Contributor/Archive Photos/Getty Images; p. 10 bonchan/Shutterstock.com; p. 11 Oliver Foerstner/Shutterstock.com; p. 13 Vardion/Wikimedia Commons; p. 14 Chris Jackson/Staff/Chris Jackson Collection/Getty Images; p. 15 Phil Walter/Staff/Getty Images Sport/Getty Images; p. 16 Michael Bradley/Staff/Getty Images Entertainment/Getty Images; p. 17 AP Photo/Jennifer Sinco Kelleher; p. 18 ChameleonsEye/Shutterstock.com; p. 20 Mark Kolbe/Staff/Getty Images News/Getty Images; p. 21 Werner Forman/Contributor/Universal Images Group/Getty Images; p. 22 Auscape/Contributor/Universal Images Group/Getty Images; p. 23 John van Hasselt-Corbis/Contributor/Sygma/Getty Images; p. 24 (top) Auscape/Contributor/Universal Images Group/Getty Images; p. 24 (bottom) ChameleonsEye/Shutterstock.com; p. 27 DEA/W. BUSS/Contributor/De Agostini/Getty Images; p. 28 GREGORY BOISSY/Stringer/AFP/Getty Images; p. 29 Brendon Thorne/Stringer/Getty Images News/Getty Images; p. 30 Tim Graham/Contributor/Getty Images News/Getty Images; p. 31 Tim Graham/Contributor/Hulton Archive/Getty Images; p. 33 (top) Rudy Balasko/Shutterstock.com; p. 33 (bottom) Andy Tam/Shutterstock.com; p. 35 Klara Zamourilova/Shutterstock.com; p. 36 (left) Shaun Jeffers/Shutterstock.com; p. 36 (right) Chris Howey/Shutterstock.com; p. 37 Gabor Kovacs Photography/Shutterstock.com; p. 38 MARTY MELVILLE/Stringer/AFP/Getty Images; p. 40 frees/Shutterstock.com; p. 41 Maridav/Shutterstock.com; p. 42 Jonas Gratzer/Contributor/LightRocket/Getty Images; p. 43 Svetlana Orusova/Shutterstock.com; p. 44 Darrian Traynor/Stringer/Getty Images Sport/Getty Images; p. 45 Michael Ochs Archives/Stringer/Michael Ochs Archives/Getty Images.

Cataloging-in-Publication Data
Names: Klein, J.M.
Title: Life and culture in Australia and the Pacific Realm / J.M. Klein.
Description: New York : PowerKids Press, 2021. | Series: People around the world | Includes glossary and index.
Identifiers: ISBN 9781725321847 (pbk.) | ISBN 9781725321861 (library bound) | ISBN 9781725321854 (6 pack) | ISBN 9781725321878 (ebook)
Subjects: LCSH: Australia–Juvenile literature. | Oceania–Juvenile literature. | Australia–Social life and customs–Juvenile literature. | Oceania–Social life and customs–Juvenile literature.
Classification: LCC DU96.K545 2021 | DDC 994–dc23
Manufactured in the United States of America

CPSIA Compliance Information: Batch #CSPK20: For Further Information contact Rosen Publishing, New York, New York at 1-800-237-9932

Find us on

Contents

Introduction
PEOPLES OF THE PACIFIC

L ife throughout the Pacific realm is a balance between old and new. With hundreds of unique ethnic groups, this region is full of **diverse** languages and cultures. Traditional dance, languages, art, and religion blend with modern life and the customs of European settlers and **immigrant** newcomers.

The world's smallest continent, Australia, is by far the largest country in the Pacific. The island is home to some of the world's oldest living native cultures and many immigrant cultures. In the same general area, three regions make up the Pacific realm: Polynesia, Micronesia, and Melanesia.

People in the Pacific realm have a rich history that has often been passed down orally, or by word of mouth. Nature and religion play a big role in **architecture**, music, and art, as well as other aspects of modern life.

diverse: Different or varied.
architecture: A method or style of building.

The Pacific realm covers one-third of the world and is made up of three regions. Nearby Australia is sometimes called "the land down under" because of its location on the globe.

The arrival of western settlers and **missionaries** also shaped the region. This sometimes led to the loss of some aspects of native cultures. However, many of the traditional practices of the region continue to this day. In fact, they're flourishing, helped by renewed interest and new **technology**.

1 NATIONS OF MANY CULTURES

Australia and the Pacific realm are home to thousands of different **indigenous** cultures, as well as dozens of immigrant cultures. In places such as Australia and New Zealand, indigenous peoples live alongside **descendants** of British settlers and more recent immigrants.

CULTURAL CONNECTIONS

The peoples of Papua New Guinea have a wide variety of traditions. Members of the Huli people wear colorful body paint and headdresses. The Asaro people are sometimes called "mud men" for their clay masks and clay body coverings. Many groups carve detailed wood sculptures.

In Papua New Guinea, members of the Asaro people are known for their masks and clay body paint. Papua New Guinea has hundreds of diverse groups.

Historical events like Australia's 1860s gold rush, the aftermath of World War II, and the Vietnam War brought people to Australia from around the world. Today, Australia is very **multicultural**. People living in Australia have come from about 200 other countries around the world. In the Australian state of New South Wales, about one-third of people are **migrants**, born outside of the country.

CULTURAL CONNECTIONS

In the 1700s, Great Britian used New South Wales as a prison colony. The British government sent criminals—especially the poor and young—to Australia instead of executing them. Today, about 20 percent of Australians are descended from these convicts.

multicultural: Having many different cultures in a unified society.
migrant: A person who travels from one place to another.

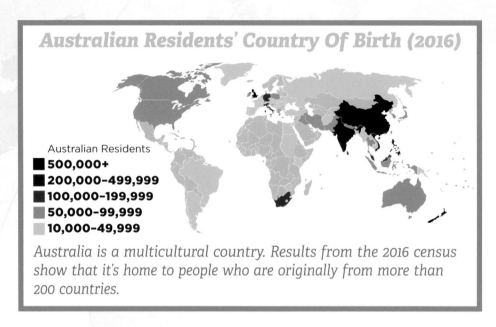

Australian Residents' Country Of Birth (2016)

Australian Residents
- 500,000+
- 200,000–499,999
- 100,000–199,999
- 50,000–99,999
- 10,000–49,999

Australia is a multicultural country. Results from the 2016 census show that it's home to people who are originally from more than 200 countries.

People of more than 160 nationalities live in Sydney, the largest city in Australia. It's home to many immigrants, including people from China, Greece, Turkey, Lebanon, and Indonesia. These people have brought parts of their own cultures, including food and music. Sydney has a strong Asian community. The city's Chinese New Year celebrations are the largest outside of Asia.

The Chinese New Year celebrations in Sydney, Australia, are an example of the region's multicultural background.

The Most Languages in the World

Papua New Guinea has more diversity in language than anywhere else in the world. About 850 languages are spoken in the country. Many people in Papua New Guinea live in isolated rural villages. Historians believe that isolation is why so many languages developed. Some languages are only spoken by a few dozen people. Today, most people also speak Tok Pisin in order to communicate with each other. Tok Pisin is a creole language, which means it developed as a mix of languages. Tok Pisin words sometimes come from English terms, but they often have different or multiple meanings.

Indigenous Huli people wear colorful body paint and headdresses. In Papua New Guinea, indigenous peoples collectively speak about 850 languages.

A traditional Hawaiian plate lunch includes food from around the world. It's similar to a Japanese bento box meal, inspired by the many Japanese immigrants who call Hawaii home.

Hawaii, a U.S. state, is also quite multicultural. Descendants of native Hawaiians live with descendants of immigrants from Europe and Asia, as well as descendants of U.S. missionaries. Immigrants from China, Japan, Portugal, Korea, and the Philippines have had lasting effects on Hawaiian culture. In Hawaii, food is very multicultural too. Polynesian staples such as sugarcane, coconut, and taro—a starchy vegetable—are served alongside Portuguese sweet bread, Japanese rice, and Chinese noodles to create meals traditionally eaten in Hawaii. Typical Hawaiian music often includes ukuleles, instruments developed in Hawaii in the 1800s after Portuguese immigrants brought similar small guitars to the islands.

People in Melanesian countries such as the Solomon Islands often have blond hair as children.

People from New Zealand are sometimes called Kiwis, after the national bird. In New Zealand, there are two major cultures: people of European descent, known as pakeha, and indigenous New Zealanders, the Maori. New Zealand's government recognizes both of these cultures. As people of other races and **ethnicities** also live in New Zealand, some people want New Zealand's government to recognize more groups. Other people want the Maori to be a completely separate state.

CULTURAL CONNECTIONS

Melanesians are the only people in the world besides people of European descent to have a significant population with blond hair. In Fiji, Papua New Guinea, and the Solomon Islands, many children are born with dark skin and blond hair, which often darkens as they age.

ethnicity: A group that shares common cultural traits, such as language.

Conflict Among Different Groups in Fiji

More than half the people in Fiji are native Fijian, or iTaukei. At least a third of the country is of Indian heritage. Indo-Fijians are often the descendants of Indian **indentured servants** brought to Fiji by the British to work in sugarcane plantations in the 19th century. Conflict between native Fijians and Indo-Fijians has led to two military **coups d'état**. Members of both groups attempted to seize power in 2000 and 2006, planning to either expand the rights given to Indo-Fijians or take them away. Thousands of Indo-Fijians left Fiji and immigrated to Australia and New Zealand, bringing their culture with them. Today, by law, Indo-Fijians and iTaukei are both allowed to be called "Fijians."

Countries throughout the Pacific show the impact of European colonization. Islands including New Caledonia and French Polynesia are still French territories and their people largely speak the French language.

2 THE REBIRTH OF TRADITIONAL CULTURES

I ndigenous culture in New Zealand has been undergoing a rebirth. Most Kiwis are of European background. However, almost 15 percent of the population are members of the indigenous New Zealand people called Maori.

The Maori arrived in New Zealand in the 13th century. They have a strong culture full of

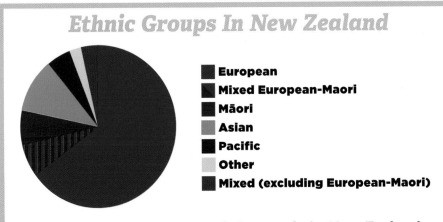

Ethnic Groups In New Zealand

- European
- Mixed European-Maori
- Māori
- Asian
- Pacific
- Other
- Mixed (excluding European-Maori)

As of 2019, about 70 percent of the people in New Zealand are of European descent. Maori, the indigenous people of New Zealand, make up about 14 percent of the population.

art, dance, and legends. However, in the 1950s, many Maori people immigrated to cities in New Zealand. Away from their roots, many Maori lost connections to their language and culture. Many people converted to Christianity. In Maori culture and religion, ancestry is important. Some Maori no longer know their ancestry or what group they belong to.

Still, in recent decades, things have been

A traditional Maori greeting is the hongi. A Maori places their forehead and nose against another person's forehead and nose as a way to share the same breath.

changing. There's been an increased interest in Maori culture. Schools now teach the Maori language in earlier grades. Many students also attend immersion schools, where they learn subjects such as math and science in the Maori language. Maori preschoolers often attend immersion schools called language nests.

Technology has also helped expand knowledge of Maori culture and language. New

The Haka

Many New Zealanders take part in an important Maori tradition, no matter what their race or ethnicity. Many people in New Zealand know at least one form of the haka, a traditional Maori war dance. To scare an enemy away, haka dancers stomp, chant, body slap, stick out their tongues, and glare or bulge their eyes. New Zealand's rugby team, the All Blacks, perform the haka before rugby matches in stadiums filled with thousands of people. People from around the world now know about the haka from watching the All Blacks on TV. In addition to other sporting events, the haka is sometimes performed at birthday parties, weddings, or funerals. The dance helps unite the people of New Zealand.

Members of the All Blacks, New Zealand's rugby team, perform the haka before a match.

MĀORI
TELEVISION
mā rātou mā mātou mā koutou mā tātou

Maori Television is helping people learn about Maori language and culture.

Zealand's Maori Television is a national TV channel that preserves and spreads Maori language and culture. It broadcasts news, programs on Maori culture, and shows for children—all in the Maori language. Studies have shown that understanding of Maori language and acceptance of Maori culture have both increased as a result of these TV programs.

Today, about 3 percent of the New Zealand population speaks Maori. New Zealanders who

CULTURAL CONNECTIONS

To help protect Pacific culture, every four years, a different country holds the Festival of the Pacific Arts and Culture. Island residents share traditional practices such as music, dance, and art to keep those practices from being forgotten.

The Hawaiian Renaissance

In the 1970s, dancing and history helped kick off what's been called a renaissance of Hawaiian culture. Once limited or changed because of Christian missionary influence, the Hawaiian hula is now a well-known dance worldwide. Each year, hula dancers compete in the weeklong Merrie Monarch Festival in Hilo, Hawaii. The renaissance also included growing interest in traditional music, language, crafts, and arts. The Polynesian Voyaging Society builds reproductions of canoes once used by ancient Polynesians to travel long distances. The reproductions sparked interest in Polynesian navigation or wayfinding, which uses the sun and stars as guides instead of a compass.

Hula dancers practice for Hawaii's Merrie Monarch Festival, which has helped spread hula dancing worldwide.

aren't fluent in the language still know many words. People in New Zealand greet each other with the Maori phrase for hello, "kia ora." TV programs and news shows often begin with "kia ora." New Zealand government bodies also have English and Maori names.

Many Maori are interested in rediscovering their ancestry. To do so, they are using the marae, the meeting place of Maori communities. The spreading Maori culture is also attracting Polynesians from other islands in the Pacific, including Tonga, Samoa, and the Cook Islands.

Maori women perform the poi dance, swinging poi balls around to tell a story. Non-Maori people outside of New Zealand sometimes use poi to help develop coordination.

3 ABORIGINAL AUSTRALIAN CULTURE, RELIGION, AND ART

Members of some of the world's oldest living cultures, **Aboriginal** Australians play a key role in Australia's relationship with art, storytelling, and culture.

Australia's Aboriginal people came to the **continental island** more than 50,000 years ago. They settled on the Australian mainland. The Torres Strait Islander people settled between Australia and Papua New Guinea. These peoples were some of the world's earliest storytellers. They may be the creators of the oldest art remaining in the world.

CULTURAL CONNECTIONS

Many natural formations, such as Uluru, a large red sandstone rock outcrop, are Australian landmarks. Many are also sacred sites to Aboriginal peoples.

aboriginal: An adjective that describes anyone from an indigenous group anywhere in the world, or specifically, (uppercase) a member of the indigenous Aboriginal peoples of Australia.

continental island: An island formed by tectonic plate movement that causes the rising and folding of the ocean floor.

A sacred site, Uluru is the top of a large sandstone formation believed to be 600 million years old.

Art and storytelling were important in ancient Aboriginal culture. They remain important for modern-day Aboriginal people as well. Early Aboriginal Australians painted and engraved rock art that can still be found throughout Australia, especially in northern Australia's Kakadu National Park. Historians believe the oldest remaining rock art in Australia is at least 28,000 years old. Engravings may be even older. Early Aboriginal artists also made sand and wood sculptures.

Modern Aboriginal Art

Modern Aboriginal Australians continue to create art, including a form called dot painting. Artists use dots, sometimes overlapping, to create a scene often having to do with stories, symbols, or the land. A similar technique was once used with sand, but modern acrylic paints make the art more permanent. Many Aboriginal artists mix the same materials their ancestors used and paint on bark. Others use modern paints, materials, and Western styles. Other Aboriginal artists use other styles of painting, make pottery, or weave fabric. Aboriginal art is growing in popularity for its unique styles and forms.

Aboriginal dot paintings are a popular form of traditional art in Australia.

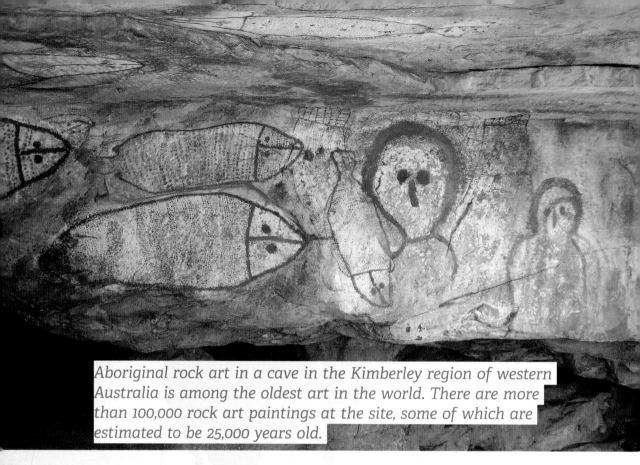

Aboriginal rock art in a cave in the Kimberley region of western Australia is among the oldest art in the world. There are more than 100,000 rock art paintings at the site, some of which are estimated to be 25,000 years old.

Aboriginal rock art tells the history of Australia. The earliest rock art is thought to be from the last **ice age** and shows a dry landscape with humans hunting kangaroos with boomerangs. After the ice age ended, trees and flowers appeared in rock art. Other works appear to show people fighting, as well as the clothing they wore and the tools they used. Rock art from the 18th and 19th centuries shows the arrival of Europeans.

The Stolen Generations

An attempt to force the Aboriginal Australian and Torres Strait Islander peoples to **assimilate** into the white Australian community badly hurt Aboriginal culture. From 1910 to 1970, government and church agencies removed thousands of Aboriginal and Torres Strait Islander children from their parents. These children are known as the Stolen Generations. The children were raised in institutions, placed with white foster families, or adopted by white families. Many children had their names changed and were taught to forget their culture or be ashamed of it. This interrupted the Aboriginal traditions of passing history down by word of mouth, and much cultural knowledge was lost. Many members of the Stolen Generations are still looking for their families.

Thousands of Aboriginal children were taken from their parents by the Australian government over the course of decades. These Stolen Generations represent a loss of native culture to many Australians.

assimilate: To adopt new cultural practices, generally from a dominant culture group.

Aboriginal peoples used tools called boomerangs for hunting. They're now important in some ceremonies.

Aboriginal musicians play the didgeridoo, a wind instrument known for its unique sound.

Aboriginal art continues to record human events and pass along stories to the next generation. But much art comes back to a key concept in Aboriginal spiritual beliefs: what's sometimes known in English as "The Dreaming." There are many indigenous words to explain this complicated concept, system of belief, and way of life. One scientist said it could only be understood as "a complex of meanings." It includes the past, present, and the future, as well as many aspects of life. This includes the creation time, when mythic beings created the natural world and many things in it. This belief system influences many parts of Aboriginal culture, including art, music, dance, religion, stories, society, and law.

4 WHAT PEOPLE BELIEVE

Traditional religions in many islands throughout the Pacific realm are based on nature and the importance of ancestors. Some native Hawaiians believe spiritual energy—or mana—exists in every object and person, and that people can gain or lose mana.

CULTURAL CONNECTIONS

Pacific myths tell stories of creation. In Polynesian mythology, the **demigod** Maui fished up the north island of New Zealand from the sea. His canoe became the south island. Maui also pulled up the Hawaiian Islands and other islands throughout the Pacific.

The arrival of Christian missionaries changed beliefs throughout the region. Missionaries came to Tahiti in 1797 and converted many people to Christianity. Eventually, missionaries reached islands all over the Pacific realm. Today, many countries in the Pacific are mainly Christian. In Papua New Guinea, some 95 percent of people are Christian.

In many islands in the south Pacific, church on Sunday is a major weekly activity. Church gospel music and hymns are popular in Fiji and other places. Christian holidays such as Good Friday, Easter, and Christmas are important throughout the Pacific. In Tahiti, churches celebrate the anniversary of the arrival of the first missionaries.

People all across the Pacific realm attend Christian church services like this one in Tahiti.

Australian Religious Makeup

RELIGION	1966	1991	2016
Christianity	88.2 %	74.0 %	52.1 %
Other Religions	0.7 %	2.6 %	8.2 %
No Religion	0.8 %	12.9 %	30.1 %

Despite common Christian backgrounds, the people of Australia have become less religious over time.

Missionaries encouraged the banning of many traditional religious practices, including spiritual dances, such as Hawaii's hula, and the art of tattooing. Missionaries called those practices sinful. As more people converted, these cultural practices declined.

Sacred Dances

Dances in the Pacific realm tell stories, but they're often also deeply spiritual. According to myth, Polynesian gods and goddesses taught dances such as the hula to ancient Polynesians. Dances connect the dancer to nature and to the gods and goddesses. Many versions of the hula exist. Ori Tahiti dancing involves moves including quick-shaking hips. A Tonga group dance, called the *lakalaka*, uses sung poetry and arm movements to tell stories. In Fiji, a traditional performance called the meke tells a story through dance, chanting, and drums. Ancient peoples sang songs and performed stories to record history and tell myths. Dances and songs today preserve that oral tradition.

Dance festivals like Heiva in Tahiti help to preserve ancient dances.

Some of those practices are returning, however. In Tahiti, interest in the *tatau*—which is the word that the English word "tattoo" came from—has been increasing since the 1980s. Tahitian tataus may show information about a person's ancestors and interests.

Remembering and Celebrating

In Australia and New Zealand, Anzac Day, or the national day of remembrance, is a major holiday. "Anzac" represents the Australia and New Zealand Army Corps. The day honors Australian and New Zealand soldiers who fought and died in wars, beginning with World War I. On April 25, people attend church services at dawn, lay wreaths during ceremonies, and wear red poppies, a flower symbolizing remembrance. Soldiers march in parades. Australia and New Zealand each also celebrate national days. Australia Day is January 26 each year. New Zealand's Waitangi Day is February 6. It marks the signing of the 1840 Treaty of Waitangi, considered to be New Zealand's founding **document**.

Service members march in an Anzac Day parade in Sydney, Australia. Anzac Day honors Australian and New Zealand soldiers who died during World War I and other wars.

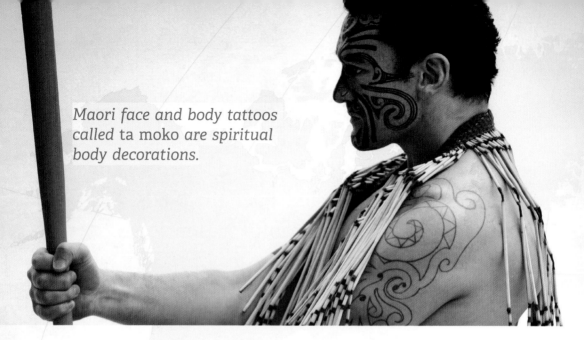

Maori face and body tattoos called ta moko *are spiritual body decorations.*

Skin decoration remains spiritual to New Zealand's Maori. According to legend, the gods taught the Maori *ta moko*, or body and face tattooing. A person's tattoos may tell who they are—their mother and father's **lineage**, their tribe, their expertise or work, and any athletic accomplishments. *Kiri tuhi*, another form of Maori body tattooing, isn't spiritual and is shared by the Maori with non-Maori.

CULTURAL CONNECTIONS

Drinking kava, made from a crushed root, is a **ritual** in some parts of the Pacific. In Fiji, kava ceremonies welcome village visitors. Kava is used for spiritual ceremonies and as medicine on Samoa, Hawaii, and other islands.

Drinking kava is an important part of the spiritual life of many Pacific Islanders.

In modern Australia, Christianity is also the dominant religion because of the influence of English, Irish, and Scottish settlers. More than half of Australians are Christian. However, religion is becoming less important to many Australians. In the 2016 **census**, 30 percent of Australians said they were of "no religion," a higher number than in the previous census.

In Fiji, most people are Christians. However, much of the island's large Indo-Fijian population is Hindu. Many Indo-Fijians celebrate the Hindu holiday of Diwali, the festival of lights.

5 WHERE PEOPLE LIVE

A region's architecture can say a lot about its culture and history. In Australia and the Pacific realm, climate and religion have both been influential in building design over the centuries. The region has also been strongly influenced by its colonial past. British influence on buildings constructed during the Victorian era, when detailed designs were popular, can be seen throughout Australia. Victorian-era British architecture is especially noticeable in the Australian city of Melbourne, which has **ornate** public buildings, theaters, and gardens often built with money from Australia's gold rush.

Modern Architecture

Modern skyscrapers are part of the skylines of large cities such as Sydney, Auckland, and Honolulu, just as they are in big cities around the world. In Auckland, the capital city of New Zealand, a tall observation building called the Sky Tower has dominated the city skyline for 20 years. The Sydney Harbour Bridge has been a famous Australian landmark since it was built in 1929. No building in the region, however, is more famous than the Sydney Opera House. With its eye-catching roof, which resembles the sails of a ship, the Sydney Opera House is one of the most photographed buildings in the world.

The Sky Tower stands out over the skyline of Auckland, New Zealand.

The Sydney Harbour Bridge stretches behind the Sydney Opera House, one of the most recognizable buildings in the world.

In Queensland, Australia, many people have built homes with large verandas, or porches, wrapped around them. They're also up on posts, which allows cool air to circulate around the house. Homes made in this style are called Queenslanders. With modern air-conditioning and housing costs on the rise, however, some people are transforming Queenslander verandas into bedrooms. **Bungalows** are also a popular housing style in Australia.

The Influence of Location on Culture

Australia's climate has an impact on where people live. Australia is the world's driest inhabited continent. Much of the land is taken up by the **outback**. About 90 percent of people in Australia live on the coast. Two-thirds of Australians live in Australia's eight state capital cities, which include Melbourne and Sydney. That number is growing because of immigration. Most immigrants over the past 25 years have settled in capital cities. People also live on the coasts because they're interested in recreation. Surf culture is a big part of Australian life, and the country is home to surf world champions such as Stephanie Gilmore. Many Aussies are into swimming, sailing, and surf lifesaving clubs. Australia has more than 300 surf lifesaving clubs, which are responsible for saving ocean swimmers.

Indigenous peoples throughout the Pacific traditionally made meeting houses and homes as **adaptations** to hot weather. In Samoa, circular open-air thatched huts called *fales* let the sea breeze through. Many Samoans still live in traditional fales, and they're considered an affordable—and fun—place for tourists to stay.

Villages in places such as Palau, the Federated States of Micronesia, and many other islands commonly have thatched meeting houses where people can gather.

Samoans have adapted to the tropical climate by building open-air fales to let the breeze cool them down.

adaptation: An adjustment to the surrounding conditions.

In New Zealand's more **temperate** climate, where people experience all four weather seasons, architecture traditionally uses four enclosed walls to account for cooler weather.

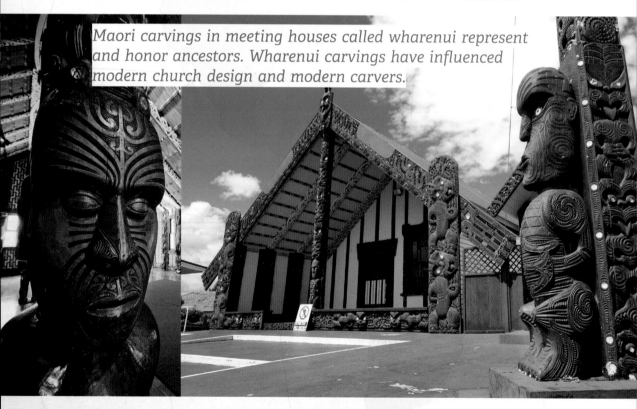

Maori carvings in meeting houses called wharenui represent and honor ancestors. Wharenui carvings have influenced modern church design and modern carvers.

Meeting houses of the Maori, called *wharenui*, are enclosed, carved buildings. Detailed carvings line the wharenui's inside walls and rafters. These designs are also found on the outside. Wharenui are important religious buildings. Carvings, as well as the structure of the buildings, represent ancestors.

Wharenui are a key focus of the marae, or meeting grounds. Marae areas are sacred places. Maori hold welcome ceremonies and formal speeches outside in a marae and host important meetings and cultural activities inside in the wharenui.

The people who carved these moai statues no longer live on Easter Island. They're a lost culture, making the statues a mystery.

After the arrival of Christian missionaries, people built churches and religious buildings with natural materials such as coral throughout the region. In New Zealand, Christchurch's Cardboard Cathedral is actually built partly out of cardboard. Officially called the Transitional Cathedral, this impressive structure was built using weatherproof cardboard tubes after an earthquake destroyed the Christchurch Cathedral in 2011.

Christchurch's Cardboard Cathedral is a unique New Zealand landmark.

6
LIFE AND CULTURE TODAY

L ife and culture in Australia and the Pacific realm are a mix of old and new. Some traditions are dying out. People in Papua New Guinea, for example, once made traditional clay pots for cooking. Now, modern metal pots are widely used, and younger generations aren't learning the traditional cooking methods as much.

CULTURAL CONNECTIONS

Because of their location on the **international date line**, countries in the Pacific realm are the world's first to celebrate a new year. In Sydney, more than a million people come out to watch as fireworks are set off over the harbor.

international date line : The imaginary line where experts have agreed each new day officially begins.

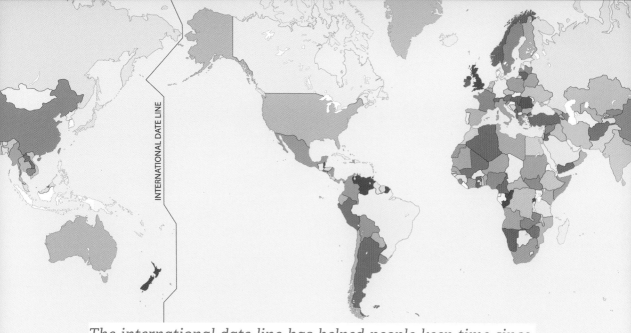

The international date line has helped people keep time since the 1800s. Many islands in the Pacific realm are located close to this imaginary line.

However, other ancient Pacific practices are sometimes shared with tourists. Fijians are known for fire walking, or walking barefoot over coals while trying not to get burned. French Polynesians are famous for fire spinning, or dancing while spinning lit torches. Both traditions used to be spiritual practices, but they've also become popular tourist attractions.

In ancient times, a luau—or Hawaiian feast—celebrated births, successful harvests, and war victories. Most modern luaus are done just for fun, often in support of tourism.

Traditions such as fire spinning have been adapted for entertainment purposes.

Some of the past is kept alive through celebrations. In Hawaii, people celebrate Prince Kuhio Day, the birthday of a beloved politician who helped improve the islands in the early 20th century. King Kamehameha Day honors King Kamehameha I, who united all the Hawaiian Islands into one kingdom in the early 1800s after years of fighting.

CULTURAL CONNECTIONS

South Australia holds so many festivals it's nicknamed the Festival State. Each March, the two-week Adelaide Festival of the Arts features hundreds of plays, films, concerts, and dance performances from around the world.

Threats to Culture in Micronesia

People and places in Micronesia are facing modern threats. Rising ocean levels are swallowing low-lying **atoll** islands such as Micronesia's Kiribati. Villages that used to be home to hundreds of people are now under several feet of water. It's believed the current inhabitants of Kiribati might be the last generation to live in the country. People are planting mangrove trees, which are believed to help shorelines and reduce the dangers of rising water levels. Many Micronesian countries have also lost significant portions of their culture due to outside influencers, such as the United States. The United States has military bases in Guam and once tested nuclear weapons in the Marshall Islands.

Due to **climate change**, *ocean water levels are rising, threatening low-lying countries such as Kiribati. People on Kiribati's islands have had to move to other islands in the country or to other Pacific nations.*

atoll: A circular-shaped island that has formed from a coral reef.

climate change: Long-term change in Earth's climate, caused primarily by human activities such as burning oil and natural gas.

New Zealand's Hobbiton attracts many tourists to the country. People can visit places where The Lord of the Rings movies were filmed.

As traditions in this region are changing or fading, the modern world is filling in the gaps. The film industry, for example, is important to New Zealand's culture and art. New Zealand director and producer Peter Jackson filmed *The Lord of the Rings* and *The Hobbit* films in his home country. The movies have increased international interest in New Zealand.

Sports Bring Unity

Sports are important to the culture of countries throughout the Pacific. Australia and New Zealand are known for adventure sports. Rugby is sometimes described as being like a religion in Fiji, and it's also loved in New Zealand and Australia, home of world-champion rugby teams. Australians also play Australian Rules Football, which is sometimes called "footy" and played with no padding. Thanks to British heritage, cricket is important in the region. People on Papua New Guinea's Trobriand Islands created their own version of cricket, combining native traditions with colonial history.

Australian Rules Football is an important sport in Australia.

In Fiji, musicians blend traditional Fijian songs with modern R & B. Reggae, rock, hip-hop, and **Bollywood** music have also influenced modern Pacific music.

Australian modern art and contemporary theater is shaped by the influence of Europeans and Aboriginals. New plays focus on the division between Aboriginal people and white people

The Australian group AC/DC influenced early rock music. Today, Australian music sounds very similar to American music.

CULTURAL CONNECTIONS

The COVID-19 global pandemic, which started in 2019, challenged the health, daily lives, and celebrations of people in this region and the wider world.

and the country's struggle for identity.

The islands and nations in the Pacific realm have rich histories and unique traditions. Though some of these peoples and cultures have diminished or have been lost over time, programs in places such as Australia and New Zealand are helping them return. As more people learn about Pacific culture, the old ways will continue to be preserved.

GLOSSARY

Bollywood: The Indian movie industry.

bungalow: A low house with one or one and a half levels.

census: The official process of collecting data about a country's population.

coup d'état: A sudden attempt by a small group of people to take over the government, usually through violence.

descendant: A person who comes after another in a family.

document: An official paper or form.

immigrant: A person who comes to a country to live there.

indentured servant: A person required by a contract to work for a certain period of time.

missionary: Someone who travels to a new place to spread their faith.

ornate: Covered with decorations or with fancy patterns and shapes.

technology: The use of science to invent useful tools or solve problems.

temperate: Having a mild climate that's not too hot or too cold.

FOR MORE INFORMATION

BOOKS:

Evans, Tom. *Myths and Legends of Australia, New Zealand, and Pacific Islands*. Chicago, IL : World Book, 2015.

Hinchey, Jane. *Pacific Islands : Discover the Country, Culture, and People*. Belrose, Australia : Redback Publishing, 2017.

Osterly, Adrian, and L. Brodie. *Peoples of the Pacific and Their Origins*. Brisbane, Australia: Trocadero Publishing, 2014.

WEBSITES:

Aboriginal Australian Culture: One of the Oldest Living Cultures
www.natgeokids.com/au/discover/history/general-history/aboriginal-australian-culture/
Read more about Aboriginal culture on the National Geographic Kids' entry on these peoples.

Museum of New Zealand: Read, Watch, Play
www.tepapa.govt.nz/discover-collections/read-watch-play
Visitors to the Museum of New Zealand's website can take quizzes, watch videos, look through pictures, and read about New Zealand and Maori culture.

National Museum of Australia
www.nma.gov.au
The National Museum of Australia offers games, activities, videos, and information about indigenous Australian culture and Australia's past.

INDEX